Circular Walks along the
Sandstone Trail

Edited by
Ruth Rogers

Mara Publications

Published in August 1994 by Mara Publications, 22 Crosland Terrace, Helsby, Warrington, Cheshire, WA6 9LY.

All enquiries regarding sales - tel: (0928) 723744.

ISBN 0 9522409 2 0

British Library Cataloguing-in-publication data.   -↲
A catalogue for this book is available from the British Library.

Whilst every effort has been made to ensure that the information contained in this book is correct, the author or the publisher can accept no responsibility for errors, loss or injury, however caused.

Maps based on the Ordnance Survey 1:25,000 map with the permission of the controller of H.M. Stationary Office.
Crown Copyright.

Printed and bound by Manchester Free Press 061-864 4540

Contents

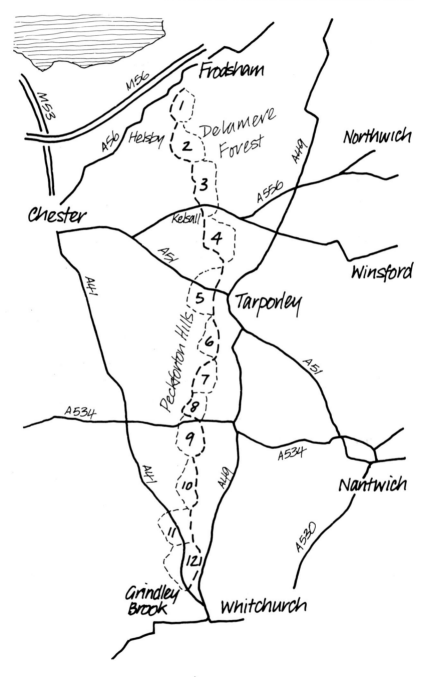

Introduction

The *Sandstone Trail* is undoubtedly Cheshire's best known and most popular walking route. It runs for over 30 miles between Beacon Hill near Frodsham, and Grindley Brook on the Shropshire border.

For most of its length it follows the Central Ridge, whose wooded, sandy slopes contrast so dramatically with the flat and otherwise featureless plain, although there are occasional departures onto flatter terrain where the ridge breaks. The final eight miles or so to the Shropshire border present a complete contrast and make their way through the quiet green pastures of Cheshire's dairy country.

Those who complete its 32 miles will be treated to a rare glimpse of Cheshire's unique rural character; from exposed sandstone hilltops and extensive woodlands to sunken lanes and oak-dotted hedgerows; from meres and mosses to black and white timbering, red brick and sandstone.

The *Sandstone Trail* has been extensively waymarked by Cheshire County Council who also provide car parks and information points along its length. Waymarking has been carried out using an official symbol which consists of a black footprint engraved with a letter 'S'. Public rights of way which join the trail are marked in the usual way with a yellow directional arrow.

The condition of footpaths in Cheshire is generally very good thanks to the work of Cheshire County Council's Public Rights of Way Unit. Away from the *Sandstone Trail* however, less frequent use means that paths are not so obvious on the ground, although all the paths used in this book were in good repair when the routes were explored.

How to use this guide

Long distance trails are now very popular and numerous walkers complete the *Sandstone Trail* in one or two days. For many individuals however, such long distance walking is neither desirable nor practical. Apart from the distance involved, motorists will encounter the added problem of returning to their car.

This guide seeks to address these problems by dividing the *Sandstone Trail* into twelve circular walks ranging from 4 to 7 1/2 miles. The average walker should be able to complete walks of these distances in about half a day. If you want a longer excursion, each circular walk joins with the previous route enabling two or more to be combined.

Alternatively, for those who want to complete the *Sandstone Trail* as a linear walk, the appropriate section in each chapter has been printed in <u>underlined text</u>. This will enable the walker to move easily through the relevant sections as the walk progresses.

Maps

Although this guide contains all the information you will need to follow the routes, it is recommended that you take along copies of the relevant Ordnance Survey maps. These will help you to identify additional features along the way and will enable those not familiar with the area to find the start of each walk. Grid references and sheet numbers are given at the beginning of each chapter.

The Ordnance Survey publish two maps which are of interest to the walker, the Landranger and Pathfinder series. The Landranger maps are the metric counterpart of the familiar 1 inch to 1 mile maps and depict roads, towns, villages and woodlands. In addition, public rights of way information is shown in a red dotted line. One sheet covers the *Sandstone Trail* and all the walks in this book :- sheet 117 Chester and Wrexham.

The Pathfinder maps are published at a scale of 2 1/2 inches to 1 mile and show far more detail than the Landranger maps. This includes field boundaries, woodlands, farm tracks and buildings. These are the most useful maps for the walker and enable the exact line of a public right of way to be followed, even where this is not visible on the ground. Unfortunately the area covered by each map is rather more limited than the Landranger maps which means that four sheets are required for the *Sandstone Trail* :- sheets 757, 774, 790 and 807.

The official symbol used to waymark the Sandstone Trail.

CHAPTER 1

BEACON HILL

Distance: *4 miles*

Section of the Sandstone Trail: *Beacon Hill to The Ridgeway.*

Start: *The Sandstone Trail begins at Beacon Hill near Frodsham. A small car park has been provided in Simon's Lane. Grid ref. 519 766 (Landranger 117, Pathfinder 757).*

The Route

1. Turn right out of the car park and follow the lane for a few yards before turning left across the golf course. Enter the trees above the deep depression of Dunsdale Hollow, turn left and either scramble down rock steps known locally as "Jacob's Ladder", or make your way down a flight of wooden steps. A well worn path now crosses the back of the hollow before rising again over a second rock step. Continue along the edge of the trees with the golf course to your left, then with trees on both sides until, just before a rock platform on the right, you can bear left over Woodhouse Hill. The path skirts the highest point which is crowned by the earthworks of an Iron Age hill fort dating from the first century BC.

This relatively small enclosure is one of several hill forts which are to be found on the high ground of the Central Ridge. They were built by Celts of the Cornovii tribe in the years before the Roman occupation.

The high ground of the Central Ridge was favoured by those early settlers because the heavy clay soils of the plain gave rise to a landscape of thick woods and poorly drained mosses. The hills on the other hand were drier and had light, sandy soils which were easier to work and not so densely wooded. It seems likely that routes of communication during this period also followed these sandstone ridges.

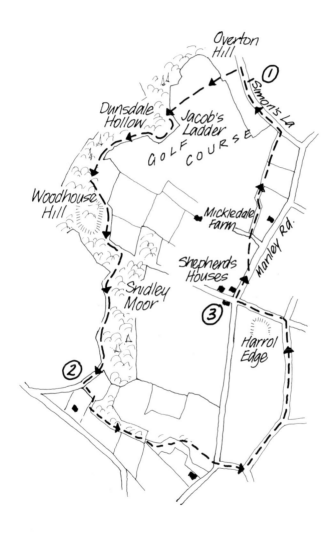

At the edge of the woods bear right keeping fields on the left, until you can turn right onto a very distinct sandy path overhung by trees. Lower down, the path joins a sunken lane with high banks on both sides. For the *Sandstone Trail* follow this lane to the road and continue from point 1, route 2.

Helsby Crag from Jacob's Ladder

The wooded area on the left is known as Snidley Moor and was recently purchased by the Woodland Trust, along with much of Woodhouse Hill. It remains as a tiny fragment of what was previously Frodsham Common, enclosed in the 1790s. Up until that time the area was primarily open heath and used for grazing sheep. The name of nearby Shepherd's Houses possibly recalls this use. Today, a lack of grazing has resulted in the regeneration of forest and scrub, although there are attempts underway to encourage the heather which covered these hillsides within living memory.

2. Turn left into a small field just before a large pond and caravan site. Cross the field and after a short track on the right bear left to follow an attractive little valley. Follow the valley for some distance until it narrows and you can make a rise to Manley Road.

Cross the road and follow the lane opposite. At the top of the rise bear left and after some distance turn left again onto a sandy track which runs behind Harrol Edge. At a crossroads turn left and descend to Shepherds Houses on Manley Road.

These sandy roads are a remnant from earlier days when the surrounding area was open common land. Their distinctive straight lines give evidence that they originally crossed unenclosed land and contrast sharply with the winding lanes found elsewhere.

3. Turn right and follow the road for about 150 yards before bearing left over a stile in the hedge, signposted "Beacon Hill, Frodsham". Bear half-right through the field and cross a farm track by means of two ladder stiles. An enclosed footpath now takes you beside the golf course to emerge in Simon's Lane. Turn left here and return to the car park.

CHAPTER 2

THE NEW PALE

Distance: *6 miles.*

Section of the Sandstone Trail: *The Ridgeway to Manley Common*

Start: *There is limited parking available on the verge opposite the track to Snidley Moor. This lies part way along a pretty lane called The Ridgeway. Grid ref. 508 748 (Landranger 117, Pathfinder 757).*

The Route

1. Walk a few yards up the lane to where steps on the right lead into Ridgeway Wood. Follow the path through the trees and after leaving the wood by a footbridge on the right, bear left along the field edge. At the top of the field keep left and follow the well worn footpath beside the hedge to Commonside Lane.

Cross the lane and take the rising path opposite which soon levels out to run below the wooded slope of Alvanley Cliff. Bear right around Austerson Old Hall to reach the road.

Although the hall appears to be of great antiquity, it is in fact a fairly recent addition to the local landscape. It was brought from the hamlet of Austerson, near Nantwich, by a local architect and reassembled here several years ago.

2. Opposite, a short field path leads to Manley Road below the steep hillside of Simmond's Hill. Turn right here and after a few yards bear left up the hill passing Manley school and church.

The study of place names can often reveal surprising details about a village's earliest history and the nearby villages of Alvanley and Manley are fine examples. Both share the name ending 'ley' derived from the Saxon word 'leah' which referred to a forest clearing. Although the land around these villages is no more wooded than elsewhere, this has not always been the case. The medieval hunting forests of Mara and Mondrem, created by the Normans in the eleventh century, are known to have covered much of central Cheshire.

Originally these forests were governed by foresters who were responsible for their protection and management. They had powers to impose severe penalties on anyone found in breach of the forest laws, which included not only the killing of game animals, but also the harming of vegetation which gave them cover. To a population who lived entirely by agricultural means, this must have been a severe hardship as whole villages, like Alvanley and Manley, lay within the forest bounds.

Austerson Old Hall

Despite this, the forest area became greatly reduced over the centuries although parts of both Alvanley and Manley remained within Mara, the northern forest, until the 1790s.

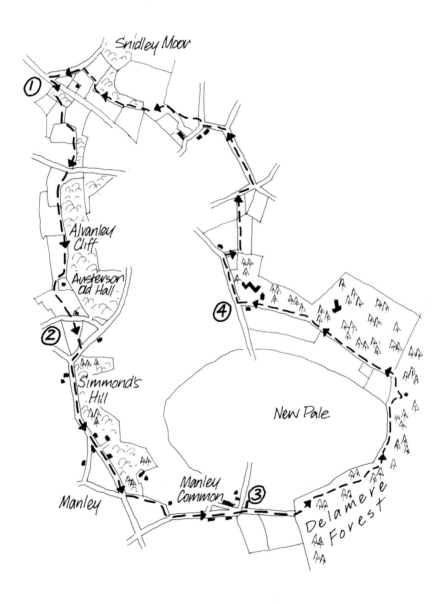

In 1812 the forest laws were officially removed by an Act of Parliament and the modern plantations were established on a small portion of the land. The remainder was turned into agricultural land and two new parishes were formed, Delamere and Oakmere.

About 300 yards beyond the church, turn left over a stile and follow the path around the field edge to meet the road again. Turn left here and continue to Manley Common.

3. Where the lane bears left by houses, take the broad field path straight ahead which leads to the plantations at Delamere. For the *Sandstone Trail* continue from point 5, route 3.

The open land to the left is known as the New Pale and is a relic from Delamere's earlier history as a hunting forest. As mentioned previously, the forest was created to protect game for the king's hunt and relied on strict forest laws enforced by the Master Forester.

In later centuries it became increasingly difficult to protect the game as forest lands gave way to agriculture, as a result, forest enclosures were built in an attempt to preserve the deer. The New Pale is thought to have originated in this way and dates from about 1617. The oval shape of the enclosure can still be picked out on modern large scale maps.

Deer were finally wiped out in Delamere during the Civil War and although plans were made to reintroduce them, it never happened.

As you enter the woods bear left onto a prominent path and continue for some distance. Turn left at a T junction and at a second junction, turn sharp left onto a narrow footpath which runs along the edge of woods with fields on the left. Turn right at a gap in the trees, then bear left onto a forestry track. After a few yards turn left again and continue past Kingswood

Cottage. Where the track bears right, continue straight ahead and take the first path on the left. Follow this path to the road.

4. Turn right at the road and after about 200 yards, bear right onto a track just before the bend. At the head of the track a stile and field path on the left lead along field edges to a quiet lane beside a farm. Turn right here, then bear left at the crossroads with a small chapel to the right and at the next junction bear left down the hill to Manley Road. Opposite, a stile and field path lead down into a narrow valley. Where the valley opens out, turn right just before a large pond and in the following field bear left along the hedge to a gate which leads onto a sandy track. Turn left now and follow the track back to The Ridgeway.

Manley Common

CHAPTER 3

DELAMERE

Distance: *7 1/2 miles.*

Section of the Sandstone Trail: *Manley Common to Primrosehill Wood.*

Start: *Begin the walk at Barnbridge Gates car park situated on Ashton Road in Delamere Forest. Grid ref. 542 716 (Landranger 117, Pathfinder 757 & 774).*

The Route

1. Beside the car park there is a prominent track, signposted "Grindley Brook 25 miles". Follow this for some distance and where the track bears sharp right, continue straight ahead crossing an old sandstone railway bridge. Beyond the bridge a dip and rise lead onto a narrow footpath beside Eddisbury Lodge. At a T junction turn left and after a few yards bear right onto a rising track. At the top of the rise enter Nettleford Wood and continue on the prominent footpath to the busy A54 and car park at Gresty's Waste.

2. At the back of the car park descend a flight of wooden steps and bear right along the edge of the woods. After a short climb follow the path between fields and enter the trees again at Primrosehill Wood, part of the Delamere plantations. Continue straight ahead parallel to the edge of the woods with fields on the right and at a prominent forestry track turn right, signposted "Kings Gate". For the *Sandstone Trail* turn left here and continue from point 1, Route 4.

3. At Waste Lane turn right and follow the lane to The Waste, a small wooded area on the left. Here, where the lane bears sharp right, take the field path straight ahead, signposted

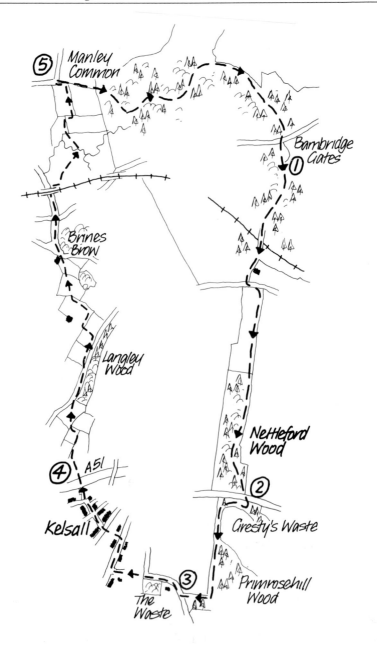

"Quarry Lane, Willington". Keep to the field edge at first then join an enclosed footpath which descends between gardens to emerge in a small cul-de-sac (Elizabeth Close).

Kelsall is a large village attractively laid out at varying levels on the steep slopes of the Central Ridge which give it a bird's eye view of the Cheshire Plain. It developed around one of the few gaps in these steep escarpment slopes, a feature exploited as early as Roman times. Watling Street, the Roman road which linked the settlements of Deva (Chester) and Condate (Northwich), passed through here and in later centuries when the turnpikes were built, a similar line was taken.

Continue to Quarry Lane, turn right and after some distance take a narrow footpath on the left (between "The Nook" and "Piccola") which drops to a stream before rising to the road. Opposite, a second footpath passes between gardens and leads to Old Coach Road. Turn right here then immediately left into Brooms Lane. Where the lane bears left, follow the signed footpath straight ahead and cross the busy A54.

4. Cut through a fruit growing area following a prominent track to a field corner with a pond surrounded by trees on the left. Bear half-right now keeping beside the tall conifer hedge before turning left in the corner of the second field. A stile in the opposite corner leads into sloping fields, bear half-right down the hill to a gate which leads onto a quiet lane.

Turn right along the lane and after about 500 yards look for a footpath sign on the left ("Public Footpath Woodside"). A gap in the hedge allows you to pass into a second fruit growing area, turn right here and follow an obvious track parallel to the road. Turn left along the second conifer hedge and where four hedges meet, turn right (keeping the hedge on your right). Bear left in the corner and look for a gap in the hedge below a solitary oak tree. Cross the stile and bear half-left through the field aiming for a gate in the opposite corner. Just before the gate turn right over a stile and pass through an area of abandoned farm machinery and vehicles. After a second stile, turn left to reach the road.

Turn left, follow the lane to Brines Brow Picnic Area on the right and at the crossroads continue straight ahead, signposted "Manley, Frodsham". After about 200 yards turn right just before a railway bridge and follow a track which passes beneath the arches of the bridge. Beyond, turn sharp right and follow a faint track which runs parallel to the railway for 100 yards before bearing left through the centre of the field to a stile in the hedge.

Bear half-left in the following field before descending to a stream. There is no footbridge here but stepping stones enable a dry crossing. At the top of a bracken covered bank turn left and follow the field edge parallel to the stream before you are forced to bear right and rise to a stile. Cross the stile and traverse a steep wooded bank for a short distance before turning right over a second stile. The path now follows the field edge with fine views to the right. After about 100 yards turn left over a stile beside a gate and make for a group of houses at Manley Common. Bear left to reach the road.

5. Turn sharp right and follow a rough track on the opposite side of the hedge which heads towards the Delamere plantations. As you enter the woods continue straight ahead on the prominent path. At a T junction turn left (signposted "Barnbridge Gates") and remain on this path for some distance. At the top of a rise bear right, then immediately left onto a sandy path with young trees on both sides. Turn left onto a white gravel track and continue for some distance.

As you pass through the modern plantation with its regimented even rows, spare a thought for ancient Delamere, created by the Normans to provide exclusive hunting grounds for the crown and preserved for over 700 years by strict forest laws.

The primary function of the forest laws were to protect game animals and the vegetation which gave them cover. This meant that the agricultural needs of the local population took second place and those tempted to disobey suffered severe punishment. This must have placed many under severe hardship as several villages lay within the forest bounds.

Delamere originally consisted of the twin forests of Mara, on which the modern plantations are centred, and Mondrem which lay to the south and east of what is now the A49. At their greatest extent these forests included all the land and villages between the River Weaver and River Gowy, and extended south from the River Mersey to the outskirts of Nantwich.

The villages around its edge must always have exerted pressure on the forest lands and over the centuries its area became greatly reduced, mainly through the practice of "assarting" or the ploughing of forest land for agriculture.

Despite this, much of Mara remained until the mid-eighteenth century when a series of enclosure orders were granted to the surrounding parishes allowing them to divide up the portion of their lands which came within the forest area. In the following century an Act of Parliament was passed which allowed the enclosure of Delamere itself. This happened in 1812 and resulted in the creation of two new parishes, Delamere and Oakmere. The land that remained was retained by the crown and planted with conifers to form the modern plantations.

Of Mondrem only Little Budworth Common survives, although there is still much evidence for both forests in the local landscape. If you look at a modern map you will notice that in the heart of the old forest area there is a complete absence of village centres, all the older settlements lie around what was then the forest edge.

Evidence of enclosure can also be seen in the many straight roads which previously crossed open forest or heath. For example, look at the way in which the line of the A49 between Cuddington and Cotebrook contrasts with that further north or south. The A54 between Kelsall and Winsford is another example. On large scale maps you will also notice that the enclosed lands are composed of large fields with straight boundaries which contrast sharply with the smaller irregular field patterns of the surrounding areas.

Just beyond a small pool on the right, turn right and after a short rise follow a sandy track along the edge of the woods with fields on the left. Keep right at a fork and continue to the road at Barnbridge Gates car park. For the *Sandstone Trail* continue from points 1 & 2, route 3.

Delamere Forest

CHAPTER 4

PRIMROSEHILL WOOD

Distance: *7 miles.*

Section of the Sandstone Trail: *Primrosehill Wood to Fishers Green.*

Start: *Begin the walk at King's Gate in Waste Lane, Kelsall. Grid ref. 535 679 (Landranger 117, Pathfinder 774).*

The Route

1. Follow the broad forestry track which descends into the woods for some distance. Just before the track begins to rise, turn right onto a narrower signed footpath and at the edge of the woods bear left. After about 200 yards, wooden steps and a stile lead into sloping fields on the right. At the top of the rise cross into fields on the right and continue on an enclosed footpath to Tirley Lane.

Continue straight ahead at Tirley Lane and after about 30 yards bear right into Sandy Lane (signposted "Fishers Green Tarporley"), a green lane which runs along the top of Willington Hill for about 3/4 mile.

2. At Willington Lane turn left and after about 300 yards, enter fields once more on the right (sign). Keep beside the hedge in the first field, then cross a stile on the skyline and bear left along the top of a large sloping field with wide open views of the Peckforton Hills and the Cheshire Plain to the right.

Turn right onto a descending farm track and pass through several fields. Eventually you are forced to bear right in a field corner following the path beside a stream until a footbridge allows you to pass into fields on the left. Turn right now and continue around the field edge to Wood Lane.

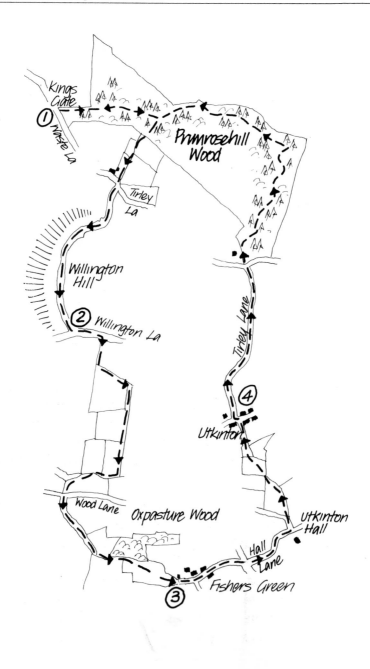

Opposite, the *Sandstone Trail* continues along Old Gypsy Lane, a rough green lane, signposted "Beeston Castle". Where the lane runs into fields, turn left over a stile and after about 100 yards, a second stile takes you to the right of Oxpasture Wood. After two more stiles bear half-right through the centre of the field to join a farm track at Fishers Green. For the *Sandstone Trail* bear right and follow Gullet Lane. Continue from point 2, route 5.

3. Turn left, follow the lane to a crossroads and continue straight ahead along Hall Lane. Follow the lane to Utkinton Hall on the right.

Utkinton Hall is the ancient seat of the Done family who held the office of Master Forester in nearby Delamere for almost five centuries. Henry was the first Master Forester, a title he inherited when he married Joan Kingsley, the heiress, in 1244. Sixteen Dones followed him of which four were knighted. The family line ended in 1662 with Mary Done, granddaughter of Sir John Done.

Dones from Utkinton Hall have played their part in several major battles which helped to shape British history. At the Battle of Agincourt in 1415, John Done fought alongside Cheshire archers, while Sir John Done, the eighth Master Forester, perished along with other Cheshire gentry at the Battle of Blore Heath in 1459.

The Master Forester's primary role was to preserve "beasts of the chase" and the vegetation which gave them cover in the king's forest. The royal hunting forests were a Norman idea and the Master Forester was rather like a modern day game keeper, except that in the eleventh century, when the forests were created, such game would have been highly coveted by the local population who were often living at a subsistence level. In addition, the woods were home to numerous outlaws, a group of desperate men who, with no right of audience in a court of law, could be killed or injured with no questions asked. As a result, there were frequent violent confrontations. Records tell of one such encounter in 1351 when Richard Done was pardoned for causing the death of Robert Cosyn who resisted arrest for killing deer in Delamere.

In the eleventh and twelfth centuries the foresters had the power of life and death in the woods and could execute felons on the spot for such crimes as being "caught in the woods with a dog on a lead" or "having a drawn bow or a bloody hand".

The severe forest laws were eased during the reign of King John and from this time on, the practice of "assarting" or the ploughing of forest land for agriculture became common. It was also about this time (early 1300s) that wolves finally disappeared from Delamere, probably as a result of the shrinking forest area and increasing agricultural activity.

The most famous Done was undoubtedly Sir John Done who received a knighthood at Utkinton Hall on the 25th August 1617 from James I. James had spent the previous day hunting in Delamere and became only the second English monarch to do so in over four centuries. A portrait of Sir John Done dated 1619 shows him wearing the Delamere hunting horn carried as a sign of his authority.

Despite this proud image, it seems he was anything but satisfied with his office for in later years he tried to surrender it in exchange for a portion of land at the Old Pale near Eddisbury Hill. This was where the foresters held a hunting lodge known as the "Chamber in the forest". Little remains of this building today but William Webb, who passed through Delamere in 1620, describes it in this way, "Upon highest hill of all and about the middest of the forest is seen a very delicate house, sufficient for the dwelling of the chief forester himself when it pleaseth him, and is called the Chamber in the Forest". A few sandstone blocks on Eddisbury Hill adjacent to the hill fort are thought to be the remains of this building.

Sir John Done died in 1629 and a year later his son died childless which ended the male line. The Forestership passed to Sir John's eldest daughter, although this was unsuccessfully contested by another branch of the family, the Dones of Flaxyards near Tarporley. His properties, including the hall, were eventually divided between his four daughters.

Turn left beside the hall and after about 75 yards a stile and sign on the right indicate the field path to "Utkinton, Quarry Bank". Follow the right of way beside the hedge, then bear left following the fence to a stile in the corner of the field. Cut diagonally through the centre of the following field then bear right and drop to a footpath between high banks. Turn right here and rise to Northgate, a narrow access road with houses on either side.

4. Continue straight ahead at the crossroads following Tirley Lane for some distance.

At a T junction beside Primrosehill Wood, continue straight ahead into the trees following a prominent forestry road. After a short descent the track turns sharp left, continue straight ahead here on a faint path which becomes more pronounced as you continue to descend. Remain on this path until you begin to rise again following a line of beech trees.

At the top of the rise turn left and at a junction of paths turn second right (the first path is a broad track and bears sharp right). This path drops gently to a broad track, turn left here and continue for some distance.

Over to the right you will see the flat topped Eddisbury Hill, site of an Iron Age hill fort and centre of the Old Pale, a forest enclosure dating from the fourteenth century. It seems likely that it was originally created to prevent the escape of deer although in later centuries parts were ploughed for agriculture.

Eddisbury Hill is known to be the site of the "Chamber in the forest", referred to by Sir John Done and William Webb. The strangely isolated location of this building can be explained by the fact that until the mid-eighteenth century the main route through Delamere followed the line of Watling Street, the old Roman road which linked Northwich and Chester. Unlike the modern route, this took a direct line over Eddisbury Hill and it was here at the highest point in the forest that the "Chamber" was built.

Take the first path on the right which follows the edge of the plantations with fields on the right. After a rise, turn right at a T junction and follow the track back to point 1.

Bull's Head, Clotton

CHAPTER 5

CLOTTON

Distance: *5 3/4 miles.*

Section of the Sandstone Trail: *Fishers Green to Crib Lane.*

Start: *Begin the walk in Clotton village, 2 1/2 miles west of Tarporley on the A51. Park in Clotton Lane beside the Bull's Head. Grid ref. 525 639 (Landranger 117, Pathfinder 774).*

The Route

1. Return to the A51 and take the footpath opposite the Bull's Head, signposted "Fishers Green". Bear right with farm buildings to the right and cut through two fields following a line of stiles. In the third field look for a footbridge on the left which takes you over a shallow ditch. Turn right now and follow the ditch to where a stile leads into woods on the right.

Leave the woods by a stile and bear half-left through the centre of the following two fields to a stile and small footbridge. Keep right beside the hedge and turn left in the following field, again keeping to the field edge. In the next field, turn right and in the bottom of the field look for a well hidden stile behind some brick ruins. This leads into a large field, cut straight through the centre of the field to where a stile leads into a smaller field. Again take a central line through the field to Fishers Green with a white farmhouse and cottages to your left.

The green has long gone, enclosed as the need for farmland increased in earlier centuries, although many of the old buildings have survived. The farmhouse, with its massive chimney, is probably the oldest dating from the seventeenth century, and there is an ancient barn in the farmyard which has a timber frame and was originally thatched.

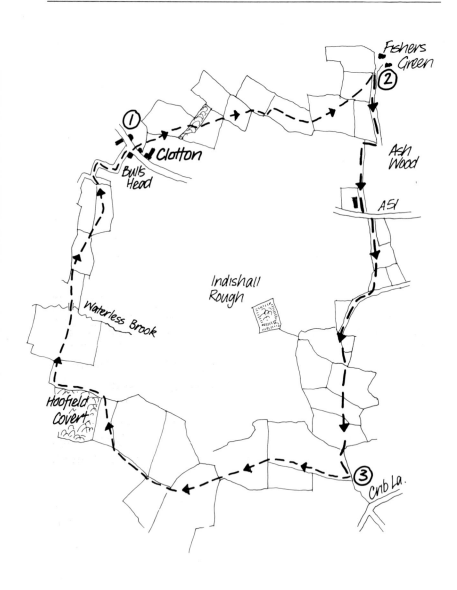

Like many dairy farms in Cheshire there is a cheese parlour built into the cool north side of the house although it has not been used for cheese making for several decades.

2. This is now the *Sandstone Trail*, turn sharp right here and follow Gullet Lane, a green lane which eventually runs into fields. At the end of the lane turn right over a stile and follow the path around the field edge to join the busy A51. Opposite, and a few yards to the left, the trail again enters fields, signposted "Beeston, Burwardsley, Rawhead". Take a direct line through several small fields before joining a green lane. Turn right here and where the lane runs into fields again, continue straight ahead passing through several larger fields with Beeston Castle directly ahead.

To the right a small wood, Indishall Rough, covers a moated site thought to be the location of the ancient Indishall Hall. Many such sites exist throughout Cheshire although little is known about them or why they were abandoned .

In the fifth field bear left around the field edge and in the far corner turn right before the stile. For the *Sandstone Trail* continue straight ahead (sign and stile). See route 6, point 4.

3. Keep beside the fence in the first large field and look for a stile in the bottom corner. Bear half-left through the centre of the second field to a gate and continue on more or less the same line in the following field passing to the left of a small pond. A stile in the far hedge confirms that you are still on the right of way. Keep beside the hedge on the right and pass through a small field then a larger one.

Here we are in the heart of Cheshire's dairy country. The heavy clay soils which cover most of the plain are damp and difficult to plough and are given over almost exclusively to pasture. This traditional use gave rise to Cheshire's famous cheese made from the milk of the distinctive black and white Friesian cattle.

Bear right over a stile just before Hoofield Covert (small wood directly ahead) and bear diagonally left through the field aiming for a stile on the right-hand edge of the trees. Beyond the stile turn left and follow the edge of the trees to a farm track. Turn right and follow the track for a few yards until it bears left towards a large farmhouse. Continue straight ahead here to a stile which leads into a large field. Cut through the centre of the field, keeping a little to the right and look for a footbridge which takes you over the curiously named Waterless Brook.

Rise through the centre of the following field to a stile by a gate. Keep to the field edge until a stile in the hedgerow leads into fields on the right. Bear half-left to a stile in the opposite corner, then keep left beside the hedge to join a short green lane. Turn left here and at Clotton Lane turn right. Follow the lane back to point 1.

Peckforton Castle

CHAPTER 6

BEESTON

Distance: *5 1/2 miles.*

Section of Sandstone Trail: *Crib Lane to Beeston Castle.*

Start: *There is a sizable car park provided for the Sandstone Trail beside Beeston Castle. This should not be confused with the castle car park which lies immediately opposite the castle gates. Grid ref. 540 590 (Landranger 117, Pathfinder 774 & 790).*

The Route

1. The *Sandstone Trail* uses a narrow footpath which passes between the car park and a stone wall which runs around the perimeter of the castle grounds. A small notice board at the car park entrance gives information and outlines a section of the *Sandstone Trail*.

Turn left out of the car park and follow the *Sandstone Trail* beside the wall before bearing left through a small conifer plantation. Cross a quiet lane and continue straight ahead following the footpath through the centre of a large field. A wooden footbridge takes you across a small stream and a second large field leads to a quiet lane below Peckforton Castle.

Across the valley you will see the crumbling ruins of Beeston Castle perched on its conical hill and viewing the Cheshire Plain as it has done for over seven centuries. It is built on the most ideal of sites, a steep isolated hill with a commanding view of the surrounding plain. Throughout the walk its distinctive outline will rarely be out of view.

The castle dates from 1220 and was built by Randle de Blunderville, Sixth Earl of Chester. For the next three centuries

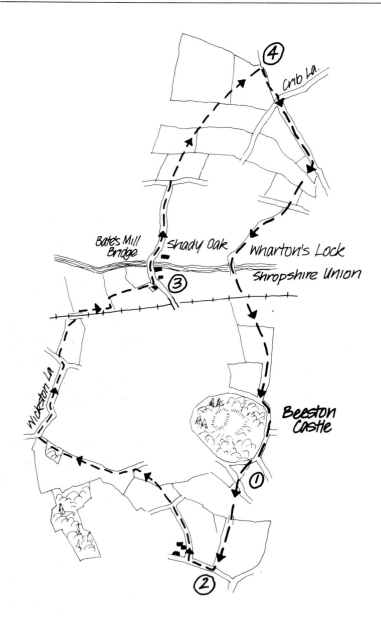

it passed in and out of royal ownership until, by the early sixteenth century, it was abandoned and began to fall into ruins. In the following century however, enough of the defences remained to give cover to a band of Parliamentarians for over nine months. In December of 1645 Royalist troops ousted them before fleeing after their defeat at the Battle of Rowton Moor, near Chester. Parliament ordered the partial destruction of the defences in the following year and the castle has been little more than a ruin ever since.

According to legend, Richard II hid valuable treasure in the 400-foot deep well in the upper keep during the fourteenth century, although searches made in 1842 and 1935 failed to find any sign of the royal hoard.

2. Turn right into the lane and after about 250 yards turn right onto a farm track, signposted "Crimes Lane, Wickson Lane". Follow the track to a T junction where a stile immediately ahead indicates the continuation of the right of way. Look for a stile in the far hedge, then bear half-left in the following field before turning left onto a farm track. Shortly the track becomes less distinct but you can still follow its line along the field edge for some distance.

Ignore a signed footpath on the right, instead continue towards a small wood immediately ahead. A small wooden footbridge takes you into the trees and a stile leads into fields once more a few yards short of Wickson Lane.

Turn right and follow the lane to a T junction with a grand view of Beeston Castle to the right. Turn left here and after about 30 yards a stile on the right indicates the right of way to "Bates Bridge". Walk around the field edge to the opposite corner where a low bridge leads under the railway. Beyond this, bear right beside the lines and at the first fence turn left for a few yards to where a gap allows you to enter a second field on the right. Cut through the centre of the field aiming for a white house near Bate's Mill Bridge.

Beeston Castle from Wickson Lane

3. A short footpath beside the house leads to a quiet lane, turn left here and follow the lane over the canal passing the Shady Oak public house. At a T junction, a stile straight ahead indicates the start of the field path which you should now follow. Cut through the centre of the first field, then in the second field, aim for the top right-hand corner where a foot-bridge leads over a ditch. Continue diagonally right to a second footbridge and half-right again to a stile in the fence. Aim for the far corner of the field now where we rejoin the *Sandstone Trail*.

4. Turn right and keep beside the hedge until you are almost at Crib Lane. Bear left over a stile here and enter the lane a few yards further on. Turn right, then left into Pudding Lane and just before a small cottage on the right, turn right over a stile cutting through three small fields with Beeston Castle directly ahead. Beyond Huxley Lane the path descends along the field edge to Wharton's Lock on the Shropshire Union Canal.

This waterway, along with most of Cheshire's canals, was built in the latter half of the eighteenth century to provide a link between the industries of the midlands and the Mersey ports. Less than a century later the advent of the railways brought a steady decline and many canals fell into disrepair. This has been largely halted in recent years by a growth in the holiday trade. The Shropshire Union Canal now forms part of a network of canals which run throughout the county known as the Cheshire Ring.

Cross the canal and bear left to a small footbridge over the infant River Gowy. A track now leads beneath the railway before passing through fields to join a quiet lane below Beeston Castle. Turn left and follow the lane to the car park beside the castle grounds. For the *Sandstone Trail* continue from point 1, route 7.

37

CHAPTER 7

PECKFORTON

Distance: *5 miles.*

Section of Sandstone Trail: *Beeston Castle to Burwardsley.*

Start: *As for route 6 (Landranger 117, Pathfinder 790).*

The Route

1. Turn left out of the car park and follow the *Sandstone Trail* beside the wall before bearing left through a small conifer plantation. Cross a quiet lane and continue straight ahead following the footpath through the centre of a large field. A wooden footbridge takes you across a small stream and a second large field leads to a quiet lane below Peckforton Castle. Turn right along the lane and after about 400 yards bear left into the woods of the Peckforton Estate, signposted "Bulkeley Hill". Follow a well established track through the woods for some distance.

Ignore a signed footpath which climbs the hillside on the left opposite an estate cottage, instead, 400 yards further on a footpath bears diagonally left up the hillside (sign "Bulkeley Hill"). At the top of the rise bear right and follow the *Sandstone Trail* through a small field with fine views of the Cheshire Plain and Welsh Hills. Turn left at the lane and at Hill Lane turn left again. For the *Sandstone Trail* continue from point 2, route 8.

2. Follow Hill Lane until it begins to descend towards Peckforton and immediately beyond a small sandstone bridge, bear right into fields, signposted "Stonehouse Lane, Bulkeley".

The bridge, known locally as "Haunted Bridge" because of the headless apparition which is said to have been seen nearby, was built in the 1850s to take carriages from the recently built Peckforton Castle to the gatehouse at Peckforton Gap.

Follow the edge of the woods for a few yards then bear left through the centre of a large sloping field. Two isolated oaks

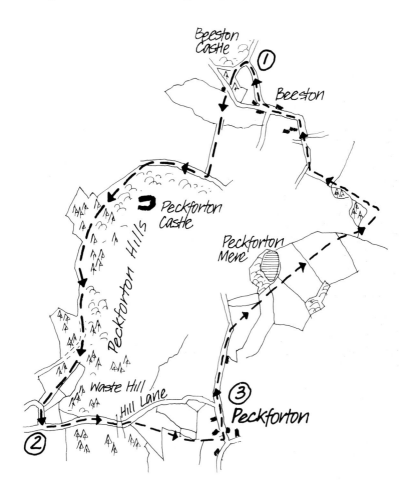

Laundry Cottage

mark the line of the right of way which continues beside a fence to a stile in the field corner. Keep to the right of a small quarry and look for a stile close to a large, ancient oak beneath whose branches John Wesley is reputed to have preached. Continue past Bank Cottages to the road in the centre of Peckforton village.

Walking through this village with its tiny cottages is like stepping back in time, yet things have not always been so quiet here. In the early 1800s there were nearly twice as many properties as there are today. One of the cottages which still stands, was previously a public house called The White Horse, while a water mill which has now been demolished, stood near the River Gowy in fields to the right.

40

Several of the cottages show signs of having had repairs or additions when Peckforton Castle was being built in the 1850s. The most outstanding example is undoubtedly the stone elephant with a castle on its back which stands twelve feet high in the garden of Laundry Cottage.

This remarkable statue was carved in 1859 by John Watson who was employed at Peckforton Castle as a stone mason. Originally intended as a beehive, it was cut from four separate pieces of stone and had a tiny pane of glass in every window. It originally stood in the garden of a cottage further up the hillside but was moved to its present location when the cottage was demolished in 1890.

The rather curious subject of the carving may be explained by the fact that the Corbett family, who owned Peckforton until 1626, had an elephant with a castle on its back featured in their coat of arms.

3. Turn left and follow the lane for some distance. About 250 yards beyond a pair of cottages on the right, look for a stile and sign also on the right. Two footpaths cross the fields from here, one veers right to Peckforton Hall Lane, while our route bears half-left to a stile in the far corner (sign "Beeston Moss, Bunbury"). Cross over a farm track and follow a line of stiles through the following two fields with Peckforton Mere encircled by trees on your left.

Until the early 1800s the land around Peckforton Mere, was a wild, waterlogged waste known as Beeston Moss. Today, drainage schemes have reduced it to a small pool surrounded by farmland, although it can still claim to be the cradle of both the River Gowy, which runs north for some 20 miles, and the River Weaver which is the longest river to run for its entire length within Cheshire.

The third field is very large and the right of way passes just to the right of centre to a stile beside a wooden horse jump (difficult to find). Head for a stile to the right of a small wood and continue beside the trees. At the corner of the wood turn left and follow the woodland edge to another stile.

Rising from the trees on the northern end of the Peckforton Hills are the turrets and battlements of Peckforton Castle, built in 1850 for the first Lord Tollemache by Anthony Salvin the Victorian architect. It was designed in the style of a Norman Fortress, common enough at the time but unlike elsewhere, Peckforton is not just a facade of turrets and battlements. It has inner and outer wards with gatehouses and a great hall open to the roof. Because of this it has been used as the setting for several television productions, notably the 1991 Robin Hood film.

Turn left now and follow the right of way around the field edge to the far corner where a footbridge takes you over a drainage ditch on the left. Cross a small field to where a stile leads onto a farm track, turn right here and follow the track to Brook Farm. Just before the farm bear right to the road and turn left. At the next junction bear left again and take the right fork by a garage. 30 yards further on turn right and follow the lane back to the castle car park.

CHAPTER 8

BURWARDSLEY

Distance: *5 1/4 miles.*

Section of Sandstone Trail: *Burwardsley to Rawhead.*

Start: *Start at the Cheshire Workshops in Higher Burwardsley. Grid ref. 523 565 (Landranger 117, Pathfinder 790).*

The Route

1. Turn left out of the car park then bear immediately right and continue straight ahead at a small crossroads. Follow the narrow rising lane and take the first turning on the left where there is a fine view of the Cheshire Plain stretching towards North Wales. Continue along the lane to a T junction and turn left. This is now the *Sandstone Trail.*

2. After about 50 yards turn right over a stile, signposted "Bulkeley Bickerton". Follow the footpath along the field edge then between stone walls before a field path leads beside the pine woods of the Peckforton Estate. Continue to the gatehouse at Peckforton Gap.

Peckforton Castle was built in 1850 for the first Lord Tollemache by Anthony Salvin, the Victorian architect responsible for a number of Cheshire country houses. This one is quite different though, built in the style of a Norman fortress, it uses local stone and has been used as the setting for several television productions.

Opposite the gatehouse, a sandy lane runs along the edge of the trees with fields on the right. Walk along the lane for about 100 yards then bear left up a flight of wooden steps which lead onto the wooded slopes of Bulkeley Hill. The path is well worn

and rises through the trees to follow the edge of the steep escarpment which falls dramatically to the flat farmland around the village of Bulkeley.

In the winter months an absence of foliage on the trees allows an extensive view which takes in much of the central Cheshire Plain laid out like a vast green carpet. Nearer at hand this patch work of fields and hedgerows ends abruptly at the foot of these steep tree clad slopes.

This contrast in the landscape has always existed. In prehistoric times when the plain was thickly wooded and poorly drained, the hills provided a lighter drier environment with thinner tree cover and easily worked soils. This made them more attractive to Bronze Age and Iron Age settlers whose earthworks still crown several hilltops in the vicinity. In later centuries, when settlers drained and cultivated the plain, the hills became extensive heaths used to graze livestock. Today, a lack of grazing has allowed the woods to regenerate.

On the steep eastern face you will see tramlines used in the construction of a water pipeline to one of the nearby pumping stations. These access vast reservoirs of fresh water which collect against the impenetrable clay soils of the plain. Further evidence of this can be seen in the many springs which are particularly common on the lower slopes.

Looking west from Rawhead

Beyond the highest point the path drops again to leave the woods by a gate and signpost indicating the *Sandstone Trail*. Turn half-right and cut through the centre of a field to Coppermine Lane.

3. The *Sandstone Trail* continues along the farm track straight ahead until it bears left to Rawhead Farm (with "The Bungalow" on the right). Continue straight on here following a narrower footpath into the woods, signposted "Rawhead". This path hugs the edge of the hillside close to fields on the left.

As you walk along the path look for a damp outcrop on the left which holds a well and weeping stone known locally as the "Droppingstone" (dripping stone). This is one of many fresh water springs which are quite common along the escarpment slopes of these hills. Also common are caves which have been cut into the soft sandstone, possibly by those in search of fine sand for scouring cottage floors.

Local folklore has endowed the caves with all manner of fanciful legends. Outlaws, brigands and hermits are all reputed to have occupied them and they have been given names to match: Bloody Bones Cave, Queen's Parlour, Musket's Hole and Mad Allen's Hole.

Eventually you leave the trees behind and an elevated path runs above small crags to the summit rocks of Rawhead, at 227 metres the highest point on the *Sandstone Trail*. For the *Sandstone Trail* continue from point 3, route 9.

As you would expect the view on a clear day is extensive and takes in much of south Cheshire, the hills of North Wales and the Pennines to the east. Further south the Shropshire hills are often visible against a foreground of rolling wooded hills which shelter the tiny village of Brown Knowl (see route 9).

4. Retrace your steps from the summit and after 300 yards follow a path which drops into the trees on the left (arrow). Descend through a young conifer plantation and at the road turn left. After about 150 yards a way-marked footpath drops steeply through trees on the right to enter fields. Continue through the field with a cottage on the right and enter Bodnik Wood. The path is well used and leads to a stile on the edge of the trees. Turn right immediately beyond the stile and pass with difficulty into a second field adjacent to the stile.

Take a diagonal line through the field with woods on the right to a stile just to the left of a large oak tree. Continue through the following field to meet the road below the wooded slope of Burwardsley Hill.

Turn right and follow the lane for about 1/2 mile. Take the first turning on the right which leads into Burwardsley village and after about 50 yards bear right again. Where the lane forks, keep left and look for a stile on the left just before a small cottage, signposted "Willow Hill". Follow the path through a small field, then along the top of the hillside before dropping to the road. Turn right here and at the top of the hill, turn right again returning to point 1.

CHAPTER 9

BICKERTON HILL

Distance: *5 miles.*

Section of Sandstone Trail: *Rawhead to Bickerton Hill.*

Start: *There is a small car park at the end of Sandy Lane in the village of Brown Knowl. This is located at the southern end of the village where it abuts the tree covered hillside of Bickerton Hill. Grid ref. 494 531 (Landranger 117, Pathfinder 790)*

The Route

1. Return along Sandy Lane, turn right at a T junction and walk through the village to the A534. Turn left here and follow the road for about 100 yards before crossing over to enter fields where a stile and sign indicate the field path to "Harthill". After a footbridge in the corner of the field bear left and in the following field turn right along the hedge with the tall conifers of Park Wood directly ahead. The right of way keeps to the left of Park Wood and eventually runs into the little village of Harthill with its ancient church to the left.

2. Cross the road and follow Garden Lane, which is almost opposite and shortly runs into fields. The skyline is now dominated by Bodnik Wood, aim for this and at the edge of the trees bear left to a stile which leads into the wood on the right. Follow the path through the trees and leave the woods by a stile with a small cottage on the left. Cut through the field to a stile then rise through a small beech wood to a quiet lane. Turn left and look for a sign on the right ("Sandstone Trail, Bickerton, Burwardsley") which indicates the footpath to Rawhead.

Rise steeply through a young conifer plantation to emerge high up on the exposed hillside overlooking the green vale through which you have just walked. Turn right here and follow the *Sandstone Trail* to the summit of Rawhead.

At 227 metres this is the highest point in Cheshire west of the Pennines and gives a commanding view of the surrounding countryside. On a clear day you will be able to see the Wrekin and Shropshire hills to the south, while the Clwyd Range line the western horizon. Away to the north the hills around Helsby and Frodsham are just visible with the massive tower of Liverpool's Anglican cathedral on the farthest skyline.

Nearer at hand, the River Dee winds through peaceful green pastures which were the subject of bitter dispute between English and Welsh during the Dark Ages. Today all is peace and quiet, although remnants of a line of moat and bailey castles remind us of more troubled times.

Below us lies another relic from those far off times, a medieval salt road. This is thought to have followed the approximate line of the present A534 and linked the salt producing town of Nantwich to the ford at Farndon. This particular road was known as "Walesmon's Way".

3. From the summit the path continues along the top of the slope before descending a flight of steps to pass a number of crumbling sandstone crags. Here the wind has carved the soft sandstone into formations more reminiscent of the Wild West than Cheshire.

Shortly you are directed onto a permissive path which runs beside conifer woods with fields on the left. Join a track near Chiflik Farm and continue to the A534 at Gallantry Bank.

Gallantry Bank was originally known as "Gallows Tree Bank", so called because the body of a murderer called Holford was gibbeted here in 1640.

Cross the road bearing left slightly and follow the lane signed to "Bickerton Church" (Bunty Lane). At the crossroads go straight ahead (Goldford Lane) and beyond the church bear right onto Bickerton Hill, signposted "Larkton Hill". This section of the *Sandstone Trail* is well used and a broad path has been worn into the sandy soil.

The trees thin out near the summit of Bickerton Hill and again you are treated to a birds eye view of the surrounding countryside. Prominent in this view is the tiny village of Brown Knowl where the walk began, along with the conifers of Park Wood and the high sandstone ridge at Rawhead.

Below us, hidden on the overgrown hillside lies the curiously named Mad Allen's Hole. This man-made cave obtained its unusual name from a hermit who was said to have lived here towards the close of the eighteenth century. The story goes that he chose the life of a hermit after he was refused the hand of the girl he loved by her parents.

The view from Bickerton Hill

Having sold all his possessions, he lived for a number of years in one of the caves on Rawhead until his solitary existence was disturbed by unwanted visitors. Presumably the cave on Bickerton Hill was better concealed as he seems to have remained here until his death at the age of about 70.

Beyond the highest point the path veers away from the edge and shortly you come to a junction of paths with a four fingered sign, turn right here. You are now on a sandy track which bears sharp left after a few yards, continue straight ahead here, signposted "Bickleywood". A second high point is crowned by the remains of Maiden Castle, an Iron Age hill fort dating from the first century BC.

Maiden Castle is the southern most of a group of hill forts which line Cheshire's Central Ridge, all but two occupying summit locations such as this. These may seem strange locations today but remember that in prehistoric times what is now the tame cultivated landscape of the plain was primarily a wild, thickly wooded and poorly drained moss. This often impenetrable jungle made the Central Ridge, with its lighter well drained soil and thinner tree cover extremely attractive to early settlers.

The tribe thought to have built Cheshire's hill forts were the Cornovii who had their capital at Wroxeter in Shropshire. Being a reasonably peaceful tribe they were easily subdued by the Romans and as a result their hill forts show few signs of conflict.

Although to the casual observer the low banks which remain give little indication of what the fort originally looked like, excavations by Liverpool University in 1934-35 and again in 1962 revealed the defences to be quite extensive. Two curving ramparts enclosed an area of 1.5 acres, while a line of low crags defended the north-western perimeter. The inner mound was found to have been up to 12 feet high and supported by drystone walling. This would have been topped by some kind of wooden palisade.

The main entrance lay on the north-east side and consisted of an inturned passage which originally had a cobled surface. It seems likely that a pair of large gates defended the entrance.

Of dewllings within the enclosure surprisingly little remains, however, quarrying activity and the removal of sand in recent centuries may be to blame for this. From excavations elsewhere it seems likely that a number of circular huts would have been built within the enclosure. These would have had watle and daub walls with thatched or turf roofs.

The name Maiden Castle has attracted a host of romantic interpretations over the centuries, however, the true explanation is rather more straight forward. J McNeil Dodgson in "The Place Names of Cheshire" *tells us that it is derived from the Old English* "Maegden" *which means* "virgin" *or* "untaken" *(untaken fort).*

Beyond Maiden Castle bear right down the slope to a level wooded area. The *Sandstone Trail* bears left now (see route 10, point 1.) but our way lies to the right where a sandy footpath takes us back to point 1.

CHAPTER 10

HAMPTON HEATH

Distance: *5 3/4 miles.*

Section of Sandstone Trail: *Bickerton Hill to Hampton Post.*

Start: *As for route 9 (Landranger 117, Pathfinder 790 & 807).*

The Route

1. From the little car park follow the sandy footpath which weaves through the trees towards the steep hillside of Bickerton Hill. As you approach steeper ground bear right and rise to a level wooded area.

The path to Bickerton Hill rises to the left from here, but our way lies straight ahead. Descend for a short distance to meet a rising track by a *Sandstone Trail* information board. Turn left here and follow the path along the base of the wooded slope with fields on the right.

After about 700 yards, bear right over a stile and cut through a small field to a quiet lane with Larkton Hall directly ahead.

It is here that the Sandstone Trail finally turns its back on the sandstone hills which have been its theme for over 20 miles. Between here and Grindley Brook on the Shropshire border lie the quiet green pastures of Cheshire's dairy country. The heavy clay soils which make ploughing difficult are ideal for the rich green grasslands which are such a distinctive feature of the Cheshire Plain. Equally distinctive are the black and white Friesian cattle whose numbers were decimated by the foot and mouth epidemic in the late 1960s.

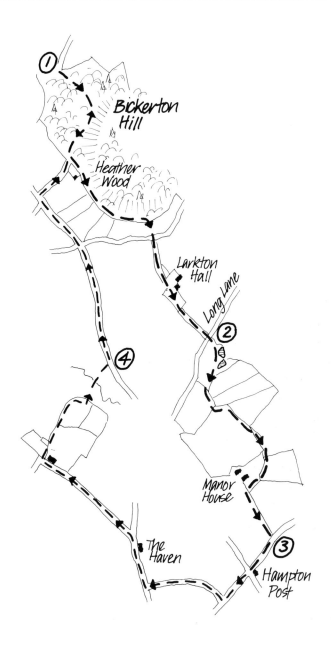

Continue along the track to Larkton Hall. Just before the outbuildings bear right around the hall to join the drive on the far side.

Larkton Hall is typical of many large Cheshire dairy farms built in the eighteenth and nineteenth centuries. The farmhouse and barns are built around a rectangular yard and, like many farms in this area, there is a cheese parlour adjacent to the main house. Cheshire was once famous for its cheese making although only one or two farms still make cheese in the traditional way.

Follow the drive to Long Lane.

2. A stile immediately opposite leads into fields once more. Bear half-right beside ponds and in the corner of the field cross a stile and turn left along the field edge. After a second stile turn left again and follow the footpath around the edge of the field until you can pass into fields on the left just before a pond. Continue straight ahead, this time with the hedge on your right, and turn right over a stile near Manor House Farm, also on the right. Bear left through a small field to a stile, turn left and follow the field edge to a quiet lane.

3. Turn right and follow the lane to Hampton Post crossroads. The *Sandstone Trail* continues through fields on the left a few yards back, for this section see route 11, point 2.

This crossroads was once on the main London to Chester Turnpike before the A41 was built lower down on the plain in 1821. This cut out the hilly section between No Man's Heath and Broxton further north. Parts of the lane are still known as "Old Coach Road".

Continue straight ahead and take the first lane on the right. Follow the lane to a T junction, turn right and after about 100 yards bear left into a narrow lane (opposite "The Haven"). Just before a sharp left-hand bend turn right into fields, signposted "Larkton". Cut straight through the field aiming for a stile to the right of a pond. Bear left now keeping to the field edge in the following two fields until a stile in the hedge allows you to pass into fields on the left. Cut through the centre of two more fields to a lane and turn left.

4. Follow the lane for about 3/4 mile (straight ahead at a crossroads) and turn right into a narrow lane which rises gently towards the wooded slope of Heather Wood. At the *Sandstone Trail* information board just beyond the little car park retrace your steps to point 1.

CHAPTER 11

NO MAN'S HEATH

Distance: *5 miles.*

Section of Sandstone Trail: *Hampton Post to Old St Chad's.*

Start: *Begin the walk at Hampton Heath, 6 miles north of Whitchurch on the A41. Park in the lane leading east from the A41 to Hampton Post, 400 yards south of The New Inn. Grid ref. 502 492 (Landranger 117 Pathfinder 807).*

The Route

1. Follow the lane to Hampton Post, a crossroads on the old London to Chester turnpike and about 200 yards further on turn right into fields, signposted "Grindley Brook". We are now on the *Sandstone Trail.*

2. Follow the path along field edges with fine views of the Peckforton Hills to your left. In the last field bear half-left to a stile which leads onto a quiet lane. Opposite, follow the drive to Middle House Farm and just before the outbuildings, turn left over a stile. Bear left around the farm and look out for a stile in the fence on the right. Cut diagonally left through the following field to a stile and footbridge below a large tree. Keep left around the field edge to where a bridge leads over Bickley Brook.

Turn right now and keep beside the brook until a small footbridge on the right leads back over the brook again. Bear right to a stile a few yards away and turn left along the field edge for some distance. After a stile in the fence, continue straight ahead and rise gently, this time with the hedge on your right. At the top of the rise bear diagonally left passing a solitary oak to where a gate beside a pond leads onto Bickley Road.

3. Turn right along the road and take the first turning on the left, signposted, "Whitchurch 5". About 150 yards along the lane bear left over a stile by a gate (signposted, "Grindley Brook"), and as you approach Bickley Hall look for a stile in the hedge on the right. Cut through the centre of the following field passing an isolated tree to a stile in the far corner. Cross the stile and bear right along the hedge to a second stile. Turn right again and follow the left-hand hedge until it bears sharply to the left. Cut diagonally leftwards through a larger field to a gate which leads onto a farm track. Follow the track for a short distance then turn right over a stile and follow field edges to Barhill Farm.

Several Roman Roads are known to have passed close to here and in 1812 an important find was made in the field to your right by a local farm-hand. It was a Roman military discharge certificate which has come to be known as the Malpas Diploma. It consists of two bronze tablets nine inches by six held together by hinges. It was issued in AD 103 to a Spaniard by the name of Reburrus for 25 years service and granted him and his descendants Roman citizenship.

It seems likely that the certificate was lost as Reburrus travelled along one of the roads between Whitchurch and either Chester or Wilderspool near Warrington.

Cut through the yard and turn left over a stile almost opposite the farmhouse. Keep to the edge of the field until you can bear left over a stile keeping to field edges again. In the field corner, a three fingered sign indicates the continuation of the *Sandstone Trail* to Old St Chad's church (see route 12, point 2).

Turn right here (sign "A41 Main Road") and follow the right of way around the edge of the field until you can bear left to St. Chad's Church.

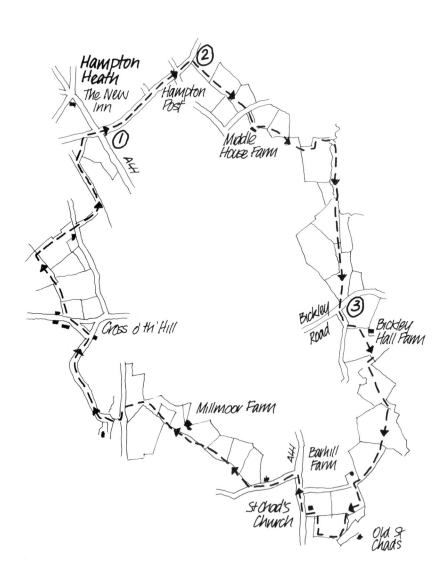

This church was built in 1863 to replace Old St Chad's which we have just passed. This ancient building now lies isolated amid the fields.

At the road turn right and after about 300 yards turn left into a quiet lane signposted "Bradley 1". About 350 yards along the lane a stile on the right leads into fields once more. The next section of the walk is part of the *Marches Way* which runs between Chester and Whitchurch and is way-marked accordingly.

Keep to field edges for some distance following a line of stiles. Just beyond Millmoor Farm cross to the other side of the fence by a stile on the right. A little further on a stile leads you back to the left-hand side of the fence again. At the bottom of the field a footbridge leads over a brook, turn left to a second stile a few yards distant and cut across the following field to a gate which leads onto the embankment of a disused railway line. Turn left through the gate and after 100 yards or so drop to a gate on the right. Cut through the field to a narrow lane beside a ford and turn right.

Follow the lane for about 1/2 mile and turn left opposite a white house. Turn left again at Cross o' th' Hill on the outskirts of Malpas.

The size and isolation of Malpas today gives little clue to its past importance as the head manor of one of the largest baronies in Cheshire. It also formed the centre of Cheshire's largest parish and required several "chapels of ease" for outlying areas. These saved parishioners the long walk to Malpas church.

Near the church lie the earthworks of a Norman moat and bailey castle, one of many along this troubled border with Wales. Today, the village lies off the main road but in the Middle Ages it commanded one of the main routes north to Chester. This followed the line of a Roman road which took a north-west line from Whitchurch passing through the sites of Malpas, Stretton (meaning village on the "street" or Roman road), crossing the Dee at Aldford ("old ford") and continuing to Chester. The lanes between Tilston and Whitchurch still follow the line of this road.

Follow the lane for a few yards and just before a cottage on the right turn right into fields once more (sign). Pass through two fields keeping beside the hedge on the left and cross a stile in the fence with a brick built cattle shed on the right. Continue through the following field and turn right by a pond (there is a small gate immediately ahead here). Cut through two fields now following a line of stiles to a quiet lane with a farm to your right. Opposite, the signed footpath continues along a farm track. After a stile turn left and follow the line of a disused railway for about 400 yards to a stile. Beyond the stile turn right and pass through the remaining fields to a lane. Turn right and follow the lane back to point 1.

Old St Chad's

CHAPTER 12

TUSHINGHAM

Distance: *5 miles.*

Section of Sandstone Trail: *Old St Chad's to Grindley Brook.*

Start: *Begin the walk at the Blue Bell Inn, an ancient half-timbered inn situated on a loop of the old A41 at Bell o' th' Hill, 3 miles north of Whitchurch. Grid ref. 523 454 (Landranger 117, Pathfinder 807).*

The Route

1. From the Blue Bell Inn turn right (north) along the old road and look for a narrow lane on the right signposted, "Sandstone Trail". Turn right along the lane and cross the new road with care before following the lane for another 500 yards. Go through the right-hand gate at the end of the lane and cut through the field to the isolated church of Old St Chad's.

This ancient church, dedicated to St Chad, was built in 1689 and was in regular use until 1863 when a new church, also dedicated to St Chad, was built nearby on the main road. As a result, the old church now lies stranded amid green fields and can only be approached on foot. The present building replaced a much older timber framed structure which may have contained parts dating from its earliest beginnings.

It was originally built as a "chapel of ease" for the convenience of locals who were spared the long walk to Malpas church which lay at the centre of the largest medieval parish in Cheshire. Today Old St Chad's still has a function as the parish burial ground as no cemetery exists at the new church and monthly services are still held here during the summer months.

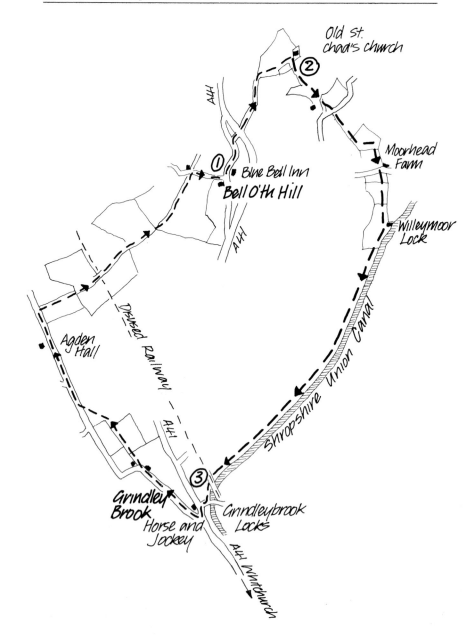

Old St. Chad's church

②

Moorhead Farm

A41

① Blue Bell Inn

Bell O'th Hill

Willeymoor Lock

A41

Disused Railway

Agden Hall

A41

Shropshire Union Canal

③

Grindley Brook

Grindleybrook Locks

Horse and Jockey

A41 Whitchurch

The small building to the left of the church was previously a meeting room but now houses an old horse drawn hearse built in 1880. It was last used in the 1920s and has now been restored.

The isolated location of the church may be explained by the antiquity of the site. In the intervening centuries the highway has shifted westwards to the present line taken by the A41. John Ogilby's Britanica, *published in 1675, shows that in the seventeenth century the Whitchurch to Chester road passed much closer to Old St Chad's, while Thomas Burdett's map of Cheshire published a century later, shows a minor road still passing close to the church.*

Many of the roads in the Middle Ages, when a church was first built here, were based on Roman roads and only in the eighteenth century when the new turnpike roads were built, did any great change take place. These were built mainly for stage coaches and gradients were of great importance. Roman roads on the other hand, took the shortest distance between points, usually following straight lines and often ignored all but the steepest hillsides. Many of these ancient roads are now lost beneath the fields although their approximate line can often be calculated with reasonable accuracy.

Incidentally, since Burdett's map was published the A41 has moved westwards again. A new stretch of road now cuts out the hilly section between No Man's Heath and Broxton further north (see route 10).

2. As you leave the little cemetery turn sharp left to a stile a few yards away (or bear right as you approach the church). Here, a sign, "Grindley Brook", directs you straight ahead and after a second stile in the field corner, a drop is made to a track beside a small farmhouse. Bear right here then almost immediately, veer left across a small triangle of grass to a stile which leads onto a quiet lane. Opposite, the *Sandstone Trail* enters fields

Blue Bell Inn

again and bears half-right before continuing along the field edge. In the second field turn right over a stile in the far corner and follow the field edge to Moorhead Farm.

Two stiles lead you through the yard and into fields again, the first is a small field, the second a larger one. Cut through the centre of both fields to a stile beside a ruined cottage. Beyond the cottage the path follows a ragged hawthorn hedge to join the canal beside Willeymoor Lock public house. Turn right and follow the tow path to Grindley Brook Lock, about 1 1/2 miles.

At Grindley Brook Lock, where a small bridge spans the canal, turn right along a short access road to complete the *Sandstone Trail.*

3. Cross the A41, bear left and just beyond The Horse and Jockey, turn right into a lane, signposted "Malpas B5395". 200 yards along the lane you walk back over the Cheshire border having crossed into Shropshire briefly at Grindley Brook Lock.

66

Continue along the lane until it bears sharp left by Chapel House, turn right through a gate here, then bear left along the hedge.

This footpath, along with the short section of lane back to Grindley brook, follows the line of the old Roman road which linked Whitchurch and Chester. Sections of the lane further north can be picked out and there are two village names which hint at its passing. Stretton, which means "village on the street" or Roman road and Aldford meaning "old ford". The "old ford" is the spot where the road crossed the River Dee before continuing on to Chester.

In the third field, where the hedge turns sharp left, bear half-left across the field to a gate which leads onto the lane again. Turn right along the lane and just before large farm sheds on the right, and beyond Agden Hall on the left, turn right onto a signed bridleway. At the end of the track a waymark directs you through a gate and along the field edge to an old bridge over a disused railway. Beyond the bridge rise through several fields beside the hedge with a distant view of the hilltop village of Malpas on your left.

Near the top of the rise a gate leads you into fields on the right. Bear left here and follow the hedge again to a track beside a black and white cottage. Turn right now and follow the lane for a short distance back to the Blue Bell Inn where the walk began.

This ancient half-timbered building is one of the oldest inns in Cheshire and appeared in John Ogilby's Britanica, *a forerunner of the modern road atlas, published in 1675. Inside there has been little change, low beamed ceilings, tiny rooms and an inglenook fire place create a cosy atmosphere on a winters day. On the wall in a glass case you can see a leather Cavalier's hat, possibly a relic from the days of the Civil War.*

Mara Publications

Mara Publications specialise in the publication of local walking guides. *"Circular Walks along the Sandstone Trail"* is our second book and follows the publication of *"A Walkers guide to the Wirral Shore Way"*. This describes a linear walk of over 20 miles between Chester and Hoylake. ISBN 0 9522409 0 4.

Forthcoming books include:

Walking in Wirral - ISBN 0 9522409 1 2
A collection of 12 circular walks in Wirral.

Walking on the Clwyd hills and the Vale of Llangollen
ISBN 0 9522409 3 9. A collection of 12 walks on the beautiful hills of the Welsh borders.

All the above publications are available through bookshops or by post direct from the publisher. Please check prices by telephone before ordering.

Mara Publications

22 Crosland Terrace, Helsby, Warrington, Cheshire, WA6 9LY.
tel: (0928)723744